AF584584

Migration to Australia

Migration From Asia

William Day

First published 2017 by
Redback Publishing
PO Box 357 Frenchs Forest NSW 2086
Australia

978-1-925630-09-1

Author: William Day
Editor: Margie Tubbs
Designer: Redback Publishing

Original illustrations © Redback Publishing 2017
Originated by Redback Publishing

Printed and bound in China by Leo Paper

MIX
Paper from responsible sources
FSC® C020056
FSC
www.fsc.org

Acknowledgements
Abbreviations: l—left, r—right, b—bottom, t—top, c—centre, m—middle
We would like to thank the following for permission to reproduce photographs: (Images © shutterstock) p9b windmoon, p11 MEzairi, p18 Peter Stuckings, p19t GlebStock, p21 reinaimaging, p23 Tony Magdaraog, p27 Dmitry Chulov, p29 Nils Versemann, p31 Thoai

Every effort has been made to contact copyright holders of any material reproduced in this book. Any omissions will be rectified in subsequent printings if notice is given to the publisher.

National Library of Australia Cataloguing-in-Publication entry

Creator: Day, William, author.
Title: Migration from Asia / William Day.
ISBN: 9781925630091 (hardback)
Series: Migration to Australia.
Target Audience: For Primary school age.
Subjects: Immigrants--Australia.
Australia--Emigration and immigration.
Asia--Emigration and immigration.

Contents

Reasons For Migration to Australia.... 4
Cambodia.... 6
China.... 7
East Timor.... 10
Challenges Faced by Migrants.... 11
India.... 12
Indonesia.... 14
Japan.... 16
Laos.... 18
Malaysia.... 20
Philippines.... 22
South Korea.... 24
Sri Lanka.... 26
Thailand.... 28
Vietnam.... 30
Glossary.... 32
Index.... 32

Reasons for Migration to Australia

Work

People have been arriving to work in Australia since pre-colonial times. Australia has needed migrants to provide the skills and labour for development since it was founded in 1788.

Family

Joining family members who have already migrated to Australia has been a strong pull factor in encouraging people to leave their country of birth.

Asylum

Wars and conflict in the Asian region have caused thousands of people to seek asylum outside their own countries.

Religion

Freedom of religion is enshrined in the Australian Constitution. People who have suffered discrimination because of their religion have found that they can practise their religion freely in Australia.

Freedom

Australia is a stable democracy with freedom of speech, freedom to travel, equality for all and access to an independent legal system.

Home Ownership

Australia has a land ownership system that gives people assured title to property they have purchased. This is not the case in all countries.

Business

Australia provides educated workers and the infrastructure needed to set up successful businesses.

Education

Australian universities and colleges rank well compared with other countries. A degree from an Australian university is recognised in most countries around the world.

Health Care

Australian citizens and residents with appropriate visas have access to a health care system which provides free hospital care and treatment by a doctor who bulk-bills at no charge to the patient.

Lifestyle

Australia offers migrants a predominantly safe and friendly environment. Its beautiful landscapes and variety of climates, from tropical to alpine, attract both tourists and people wanting to settle permanently.

Top 10 Countries of Birth in Australia (2015)

Country of birth	Number of migrants	% of the Australian population
United Kingdom	1,207,000	5.1%
New Zealand	611,400	2.6%
China	481,800	2.0%
India	432,700	1.8%
Philippines	236,400	1.0%
Vietnam	230,200	1.0%
Italy	198,200	0.8%
South Africa	178,700	0.8%
Malaysia	156,500	0.7%
Germany	125,900	0.5%

In 2016, 28% of Australia's population were born overseas.

Cambodia

The capital city of Cambodia is Phnom Penh.

From the early 1950s, small numbers of Cambodian students arrived in Australia under the Colombo Plan. After the Khmer Rouge took control of Cambodia in 1975, Cambodians escaping the tyrannical regime went to many countries, including Australia.

The largest numbers of people with Cambodian heritage live in Victoria and New South Wales. Buddhism is the religion followed by the majority of these migrants. The Cambodian Buddhist temple, Wat Khemarangsaram, was built by the Sydney community. The temple is the focus for Khmer New Year celebrations held in April.

Indochina

Indochina refers to these countries: Vietnam, Laos and Cambodia. They are grouped together because of their shared history as French colonies.

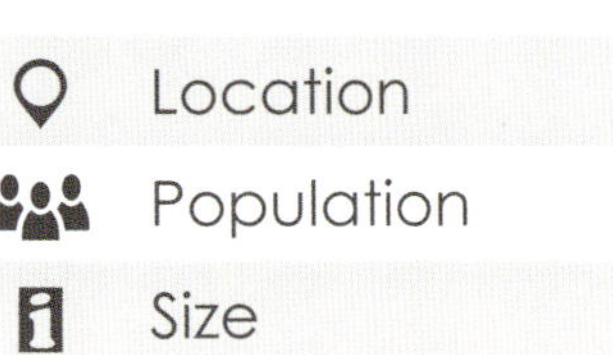
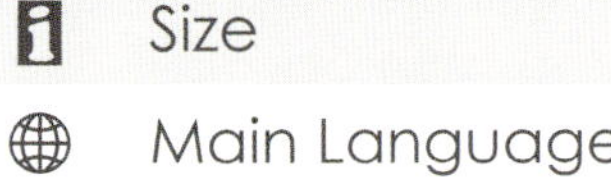

	Cambodia	Australia
Location	Eastern Asia	South Pacific region (Oceania)
Population	16 million	24 million
Size	177,00 square kilometres	7.6 million square kilometres
Main Languages	Khmer	English

China

The capital city of China is Beijing.

	China	Australia
Location	Eastern Asia	South Pacific region (Oceania)
Population	1.4 billion	24 million
Size	9.3 million square kilometres	7.6 million square kilometres
Main Languages	Mandarin, Cantonese	English

Colonial Era

Chinese people have been arriving in Australia since the early days of the colonies. There is a long tradition of Chinese sailors leaving their villages in the south of China and travelling to find work in Australia. The gold rush of the 1850s was a strong pull factor for Chinese migrants.

In 1861, Chinese people were the second largest immigrant group after the British.

World War II

Before and during World War II, Japan invaded China and occupied the coastal cities. Chinese people who were visiting Australia, or who were sailors on merchant ships, could not go home so became refugees.

Although Australia had a White Australia Policy at the time, which restricted the arrival of people based on their race, the government allowed these Chinese refugees to stay in Australia temporarily. China was an ally of Australia during this war, and the Chinese sailors were expected to help in the defence of Australia. They worked in factories that made equipment for the war and served on the naval convoys that supplied the food and ammunition needed by Australian soldiers fighting in the Pacific region. On their shore leave, the Chinese sailors, many of whom were accustomed to a western style of life, started social groups which included European Australians. The annual Dragon Ball was a formal social event that continued for many years in Sydney after the war.

When food rationing had to be introduced for everyone during World War II in Australia, some people with Chinese heritage were allowed an extra ration of rice.

After the war ended in 1945, most of the Chinese refugees had to return to China. A few were allowed to stay in Australia, where they started families and ran successful businesses.

People's Republic of China

When the People's Republic of China was established in 1949, Chinese people who had not supported the communist movement feared for their safety. Some managed to escape and sought asylum in Australia. For many years, the People's Republic of China would not permit its citizens to emigrate.

In 1989, the Chinese government used tanks and soldiers to stop a large protest held in Tiananmen Square in Beijing. As a result of this action, Australia received thousands of requests for asylum from Chinese students who were studying in Australia.

Chinatowns

The Chinatowns that developed in cities around Australia were initially places where people with Chinese heritage could gather and buy the imported goods and foods that were not on sale in any other shops. Today, these Chinatowns are major tourist attractions, with vibrant and colourful shops and restaurants.

Recent Migration

Recent skilled migration from China has brought many professional and business people to Australia. While migrants from southern China were the most numerous in the past, people from central and northern China are now also settling in Australia. China is the third largest source of migrants to Australia.

Chinese Culture

Food

Chinese restaurants provided Australians with their first widespread introduction to a style of cooking that was very different from that found in Britain. Chillies, hot spices and soy sauce are common ingredients in meals today, but they were unknown in most households across Australia before the 1970s.

Religion

Chinese people have a number of religions including Buddhism, Christianity and Taoism. Historic Buddhist temples throughout Australia are fascinating reminders of the way of life of Chinese migrants in colonial times. The Nan Tien Temple near Wollongong in New South Wales is the largest Buddhist temple in the southern hemisphere. It was opened in 1995.

Festivals

Chinese New Year	The date of this traditional spring festival changes each year.
Mid-Autumn Festival	Moon cakes are the traditional food for this lunar festival.
Qingming Festival	Held in April as a day to remember ancestors.
Dragon Boat Festival	Although held in May in China, traditional Dragon Boat races are held to coincide with other Chinese festivals in Australia.

Dragon Dance

The Dragon Dance is a performance in which a long dragon made of fabric is carried through streets and around buildings to bring good luck to an area. Dragons are symbols of good fortune in Chinese culture and the Dragon Dance appears in many Chinese festivals.

East Timor

The capital city of East Timor is Dili.

East Timor was a former Portuguese colony, later occupied by Indonesia before gaining independence in 2002. The war that occurred before this led to thousands of refugees from East Timor arriving in Australia. Australian defence forces assisted the East Timorese people during this difficult time, and the first President of the newly-independent nation had close ties with Australia.

Apart from the refugees who escaped the conflict over independence, a few hundred people from East Timor also arrived in Australia during World War II.

East Timorese people are mostly Roman Catholic, due to their country's long history as a Portuguese colony. The majority of East Timorese migrants live in Victoria.

	East Timor	Australia
 Location	Southeast Asia	South Pacific region (Oceania)
 Population	1.2 million	24 million
 Size	15,000 square kilometres	7.6 million square kilometres
 Main Languages	Portuguese, Tetum	English

Challenges Faced by Migrants

Shopping

When a person cannot understand English well, grocery shopping can be stressful.

Health Care

Working out where to go for a health problem can be difficult when a person is not familiar with their surroundings.

Family

Not having any family nearby can make people feel lonely and isolated.

Lifestyle

Ways of living that are normal in one country may be criticised in others.

Education

Educational qualifications achieved in another country are not always recognised in Australia.

Emergencies

Seeking help in an emergency can be difficult if a person does not speak English well and does not know about the services available.

Legal System

Becoming familiar with Australia's legal system is a challenge to new migrants.

Transport

People need to work out how to use public and private transport without getting lost. This is complicated if a person has difficulty reading signs written in English.

India

The capital city of India is New Delhi.

Colonial Era

Indian sailors probably came to Australia in pre-colonial times, working on trading ships that visited the northern coast. After the colony of New South Wales was founded in 1788, there was regular trade between Calcutta in India and Sydney. Most of the colony's imported fabrics, rice and lentils came from India.

Men from northern India came to Australia in the 1800s as cameleers. Using camels for transport, they provided the delivery services for much of inland Australia.

Britain was a colonial power in India during the 1800s and up until 1947, when India gained independence. This long history of interaction with the British means that Indian migrants to Australia find themselves in a society that is familiar in many ways.

Before the White Australia Policy imposed restrictions, a number of Sikh people came from India to work in country areas. Their descendants have formed a sizeable Sikh community in Woolgoolga, New South Wales.

People Today

India is the fourth largest source of migrants to Australia. The level of tertiary education among people with Indian heritage in Australia is statistically higher than that of the total Australian population.

BRIDGE Project

The BRIDGE project aims to develop cultural awareness by training teachers and encouraging contact between schools across Asia and in Australia. The project is supported by the Australian government's aid program and runs in conjunction with the Asia Education Foundation.

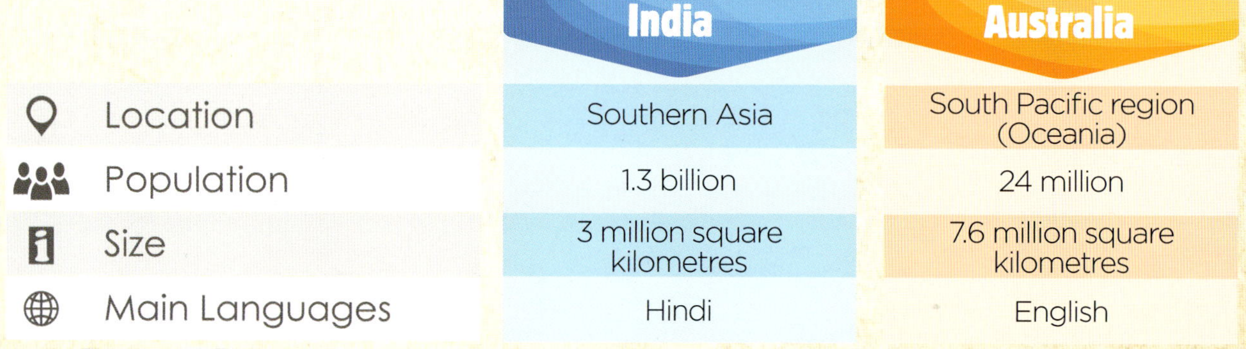

	India	Australia
Location	Southern Asia	South Pacific region (Oceania)
Population	1.3 billion	24 million
Size	3 million square kilometres	7.6 million square kilometres
Main Languages	Hindi	English

Indian Culture

Food

Tandoori, tikka, naan and chapatti are words for popular Indian foods and the terms are now easily understood by most people in Australia. Vegetarianism is common among Indian people for religious reasons.

Religion

Most Indian people are Hindu, although there are also many Muslims, Christians, Sikhs and Buddhists. The Sri Durga Temple near Melbourne is Australia's largest Hindu temple. It was opened in 2015.

Festivals

Diwali This joyous festival, also known as the Festival of Lights, celebrates the triumph of good over evil and light over darkness. Indian people celebrate Diwali each October in Australia by exchanging gifts, enjoying sweet treats, decorating their houses and celebrating with family and friends.

Holi The Holi festival (also known as 'festival of colours' and 'festival of love') is celebrated in India by people happily tossing coloured water and powder over each other. Held in March, it originated thousands of years ago as a spring festival.

Indonesia

The capital city of Indonesia is Jakarta.

Colonial Era

Indonesian sailors visited Australia's northern coast long before colonisation in 1788. They traded with the local Aboriginal people, who painted pictures of their boats as rock art. Called Macassans in early European records, the Indonesians gathered the trepang from Australia's northern waters for many hundreds of years. In the mid-1800s, people from Indonesia worked in Australia's sugar cane industry and as pearl divers.

20th Century

Australia accepted temporary Indonesian refugees in 1942, when Japan invaded their country. With the removal of the White Australia Policy in 1975, migrants from Indonesia began to arrive under the skilled migration scheme.

People Today

The largest population of Indonesian migrants lives in New South Wales.

Religion

The majority of Indonesian people in Indonesia are Muslims. Because of the large number of ethnic Chinese who have emigrated from Indonesia, Christianity is more common among people of Indonesian heritage in Australia.

Relationship With Australia

Indonesia is Australia's northern neighbour. There are strong ties between the two nations in the areas of defence, trade, aid and cultural exchange. The Australia Indonesia Centre has been in operation since 2014. Its aim is to build relationships, knowledge and understanding by conducting research and providing leadership. Initiatives for young people include the Australia-Indonesia Youth Association, and the National Australia Indonesia Language Awards, which promote Indonesian language study in Australia.

	Indonesia	Australia
Location	Southeast Asia	South Pacific region (Oceania)
Population	258 million	24 million
Size	1.8 million square kilometres	7.6 million square kilometres
Main Languages	Bahasa Indonesia	English

Association of Southeast Asian Nations (ASEAN)

ASEAN was founded in 1967 by Indonesia, Malaysia, the Philippines, Singapore and Thailand. ASEAN's purpose is to promote political, economic and social cooperation and regional stability. Brunei, Vietnam. Laos, Burma and Cambodia joined later, bringing the total membership to ten. ASEAN's headquarters are in Jakarta, Indonesia. There are 620 million people in Southeast Asia. The region is important to Australia for trade, investment, tourism, education and migration.

inatown, Melbourne

Japan

The capital city of Japan is Tokyo.

Colonial Era

A small number of Japanese people arrived in the Australian colonies before Federation. By 1879, there were enough people to warrant the appointment of an Honorary Consul for Japan in Melbourne.

Pearl Industry

The Japanese pearl divers were vital to the pearling industry in Broome, where there is an historic Japanese cemetery. Japanese people later developed the cultured pearl industry in the area.

World War II

During World War II, people of Japanese descent in Australia were sent to internment camps. Japanese prisoners of war were also sent to camps throughout Australia. A mass breakout from the Cowra Prisoner of War camp in 1944 resulted in many deaths and injuries.

After the war ended in 1945, Japanese 'war brides' were allowed to come to Australia, despite the White Australia Policy being in force at the time.

People Today

Today, people from Japan work for the Australian divisions of Japanese multinational corporations. Migrants from Japan are also known for their involvement in the professions, small businesses and restaurants, with most of them settling in Queensland and New South Wales.

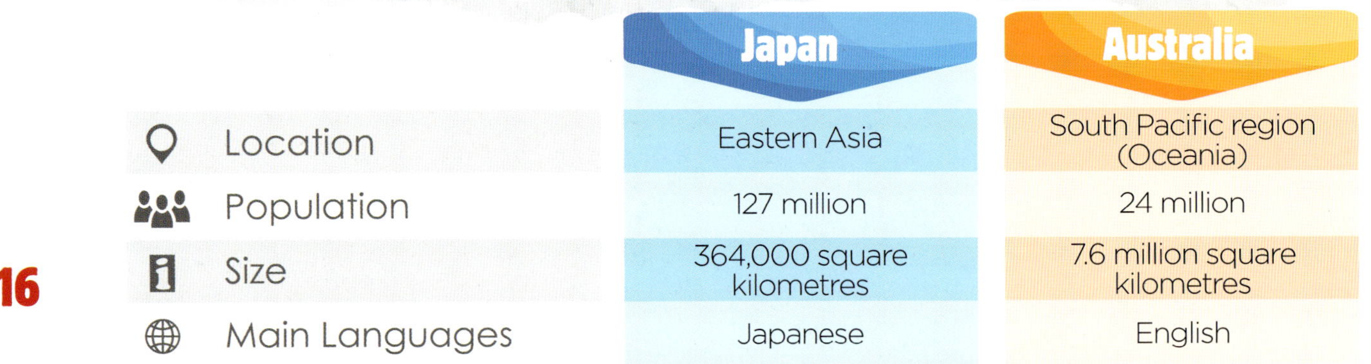

	Japan	Australia
Location	Eastern Asia	South Pacific region (Oceania)
Population	127 million	24 million
Size	364,000 square kilometres	7.6 million square kilometres
Main Languages	Japanese	English

Japanese Culture

Food

Sushi, raw fish, raw beef, miso and tempura are now favourites for customers in Australia's Japanese restaurants. Their popularity is a recent phenomenon. Unused to eating foods from different cultures, Australians once would not consider eating raw fish or meat. The expansion in the range of foods available in Australian cities has now changed this attitude. Australians have become a nation that enjoys eating the best from cuisines around the world.

Religion

The two main religions in Japan are Shinto and Buddhism. Shinto is an ancient religion in which gods represent nature and the land is revered.

Warriors

Ninja and Samurai warriors are now familiar to people in Australia through their depiction in movies and novels. They lived according to strict rules which stressed bravery and obedience to codes of conduct, both in battle and in daily life.

Laos

The capital city of Laos is Vientiane.

The kingdom of Lao was established in the 14th century and lasted in various forms right up until 1975. Lao people have come to Australia under the Colombo Plan, and also after the 1975 establishment of the communist government. Today, family reunion is the main basis for migration.

Religion

Buddhists form the largest religious group among Lao people. Despite their relatively small numbers in Australia, people of Laotian heritage have contributed to the building of a number of Buddhist temples where they can meet and practise their religion.

Festival

The Lao New Year, Song Kan, is held in April. Customs include young people throwing water over each other and the reverent bathing of statues of the Buddha, as a way of promoting good fortune.

Lao people throw water on each other as part of the New Year festival

	Laos	Australia
Location	Southeast Asia	South Pacific region (Oceania)
 Population	7 million	24 million
 Size	231,000 square kilometres	7.6 million square kilometres
 Main Languages	Lao, French, English	English

World Cultures

World cultures are divided by using terms that include:

Western, Eastern, Middle Eastern, Near Eastern, Asian, Polynesian

These adjectives refer to a lifestyle rather than a strictly-defined geographical region. At different times throughout history, some countries have been described by one or more of these terms.

Australia is called a 'western' country because of the way people live and the style of government, even though it is nowhere near western Europe.

Malaysia

The capital city of Malaysia is Kuala Lumpur.

Colonial Era

The country now called Malaysia was a British colony in the 18th and 19th centuries, when it was called the Malay Peninsula. Malaysia was formed after independence in 1963.

In the colonial era, Malay men sailed to Australia to take up work as pearl divers and agricultural labourers. They were also involved in the trepang trade, which they conducted along the northern coast for hundreds of years before the British claimed Australia.

World War II

During World War II, a few Malaysian refugees were given asylum in Australia after Japan invaded their country. Most of the migrants at this time were European people who had been living in Malaysia.

People Today

Today, Malaysian migrants to Australia arrive under the family reunion or skilled migration schemes. According to the Australian Bureau of Statistics, Malaysians form the ninth largest migrant group in Australia. Their largest communities are in Victoria, New South Wales and Western Australia.

Religion

Malaysian migrants in Australia are mostly Buddhists and Christians, because of their ethnic Chinese heritage. However, the majority of people in Malaysia are Muslims.

Business

Australia and Malaysia have extensive business ties, encouraged by the governments of both countries, private business organisations and the recent free-trade agreement. Malaysian migrants in Australia play a vital role in supporting trade between the two nations, which is valued at over $19 billion per annum.

	Malaysia	Australia
Location	Southeast Asia	South Pacific region (Oceania)
Population	31 million	24 million
Size	329,000 square kilometres	7.6 million square kilometres
Main Languages	Bahasa Malaysia	English

Education

In recent years, thousands of Malaysian students have attended Australian universities and colleges. Three Australian universities have opened campuses in Malaysia, to cater for the high demand for Australian education.

Monash University in Malaysia

Philippines

The capital city of the Philippines is Manila.

Reasons for Migration

A few Filipino people worked as pearl divers in Western Australia in the 1870s. Much later, in the 1940s, Filipino people arrived in Australia to escape the Japanese occupation of the Philippines during World War II. Political unrest in the 1970s also resulted in Filipino people seeking to migrate to Australia.

The majority of people with Filipino heritage in Australia live in New South Wales and Victoria. Recent migrants have arrived as part of family reunion or skilled migration schemes. They form the fifth largest migrant group in Australia.

Filipino Culture

Religion

About three quarters of people with Filipino heritage in Australia are Roman Catholics.

Festivals

The Christian festivals of Christmas and Easter are celebrated in the Philippines over many days, with great excitement, devotion and happiness. Christmas lanterns, called parols, are seen everywhere and used widely as a symbol of the religious season. They are star shaped and hung outside homes and businesses. The Christian religious traditions of the Philippines are a result of the country being a Spanish colony for over three hundred years, from the 16th century until 1898.

Christmas parol/lantern

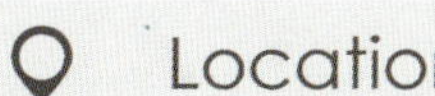

	Philippines	Australia
Location	Southeast Asia	South Pacific region (Oceania)
Population	103 million	24 million
Size	298,000 square kilometres	7.6 million square kilometres
Main Languages	Filipino, English	English

South Korea

The capital city of South Korea is Seoul.

History

Japan colonised Korea from 1910 until the end of World War II in 1945. The country was then divided into north and south. Soldiers from both sides now patrol the border and people are not allowed to cross between North and South Korea.

The Korean War (1950-1953) was fought to stop North Korean forces taking control of South Korea. Australian troops participated in this war, in support of the South Koreans.

Skilled migrants from South Korea first arrived in 1969. From the 1970s, more Korean people settled in Australia, including family members sponsored under family reunion schemes. The majority of people with Korean heritage have settled in New South Wales.

People Today

South Korea has made enormous economic progress in recent years and is now Australia's fourth largest source of goods and services. Korean investment in Australian property and mining has brought many South Korean business people to Australia.

Religion

Christianity and Buddhism are the largest religions in South Korea, but Christians outnumber other religions among the migrants to Australia.

	South Korea	Australia
Location	Eastern Asia	South Pacific region (Oceania)
Population	51 million	24 million
Size	97,000 square kilometres	7.6 million square kilometres
Main Languages	Korean, English	English

Workers and Skilled Migration

Australia has always needed to import workers. Initially, labour was provided by convicts but, after the late 1860s, they were no longer sent to Australia. The small population of Australia meant that there were not enough workers for farms, shops and industries.

Mass immigration programs were devised to encourage British and other European people to migrate to Australia. Despite these colonial migration schemes, there were still not enough workers. Up until 1901, when the White Australia Policy came into force, people from non-European countries were also allowed to come to Australia to work.

After World War II, another mass migration scheme from Europe provided the workers Australia lacked.

The selection of migrants to Australia today is based on hundreds of work categories for which there are not enough local skilled people to fill the available jobs. These categories change as the economy grows or contracts.

Sri Lanka

The capital of Sri Lanka is Sri Jayawardenepura Kotte, a suburb of the commercial capital and largest city, Colombo. The island of Ceylon changed its name to Sri Lanka in 1972.

History

In 1901, there were about 600 Sri Lankan people living in Australia, where they worked in pearling and agriculture. From the 1970s, migrants from Sri Lanka have included Tamils, Sinhalese and Burghers (people of European descent).

The Sri Lankan Civil War, between the Tamil militants and the government, began in 1983. It resulted in many Sri Lankan asylum seekers leaving their country.

People Today

Recent Sri Lankan migrants have arrived under family reunion and skilled migration schemes. The largest Sri Lankan communities in Australia are in New South Wales and Victoria.

Religion

Most people of Sri Lankan heritage in Australia are Buddhists, Christians or Hindus.

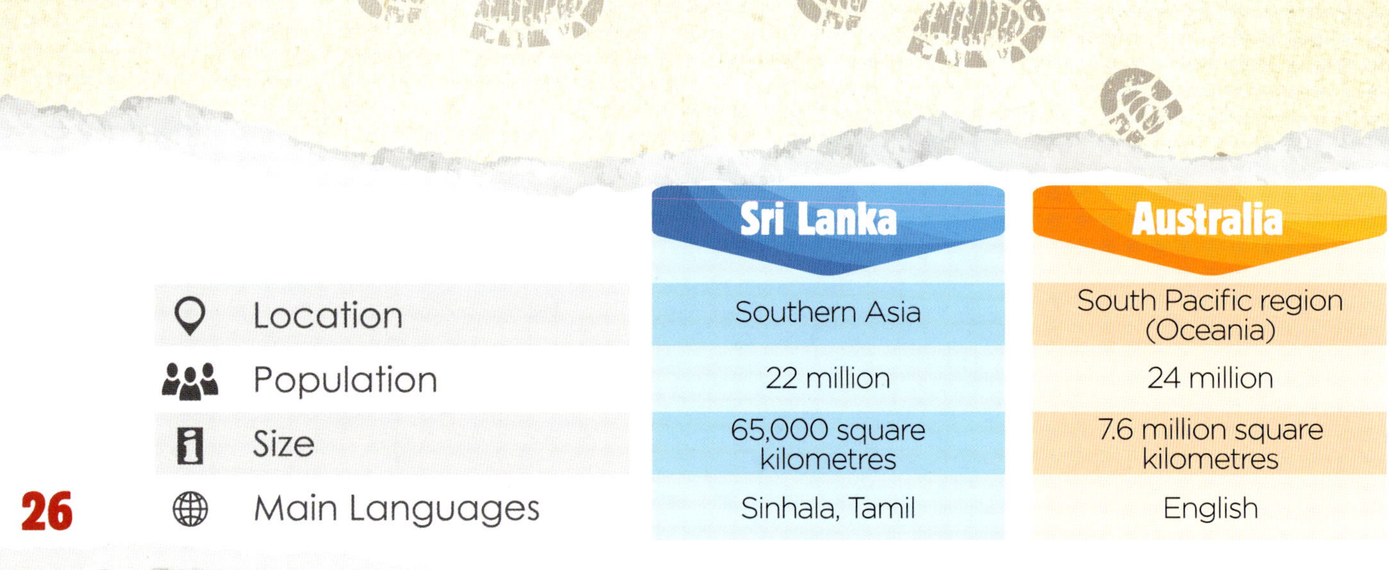

	Sri Lanka	Australia
Location	Southern Asia	South Pacific region (Oceania)
Population	22 million	24 million
Size	65,000 square kilometres	7.6 million square kilometres
Main Languages	Sinhala, Tamil	English

Colombo Plan

The Colombo Plan was formed in 1950 by a group of Commonwealth countries, including Australia. The aim was to assist development in Southeast Asia.

Under this plan, Australia offered places in universities to students from Southeast Asia. These young people were often housed with Australian families who had not had any regular contact with Asian people before, resulting in a broadening of cultural understanding on both sides.

New Colombo Plan

Since 2015, scholarships have been awarded to Australians to study in countries across the Indo-Pacific region, reversing the flow of students which occurred under the original Colombo Plan.

Colombo Sri Lanka

Thailand

The capital city of Thailand is Bangkok.

History

Known as Siam until 1939, the kingdom of Thailand was founded in the 14th century. It is the only Southeast Asian country never colonised by Europeans. In the early 1900s, the King of Siam sent emissaries to Australia to further his country's awareness and to acquire racehorses.

People Today

Many Thai migrants to Australia initially arrived as students, or under family reunion or skilled migration schemes. New South Wales has the largest number of people with Thai heritage, followed by Victoria and Queensland.

Thai Australians maintain a deep respect for their King, and frequently keep a portrait of him in their homes or businesses.

Food

Thai food has become one of Australia's most popular cuisines. Royal Thai cuisine is a style of food preparation that developed in the royal palaces. It involves perfect presentation, great attention to detail, and a fine balance of flavours.

Religion

The majority of Thais are Buddhists and there are temples in every state of Australia. As well as providing places of worship, the temples are also cultural centres.

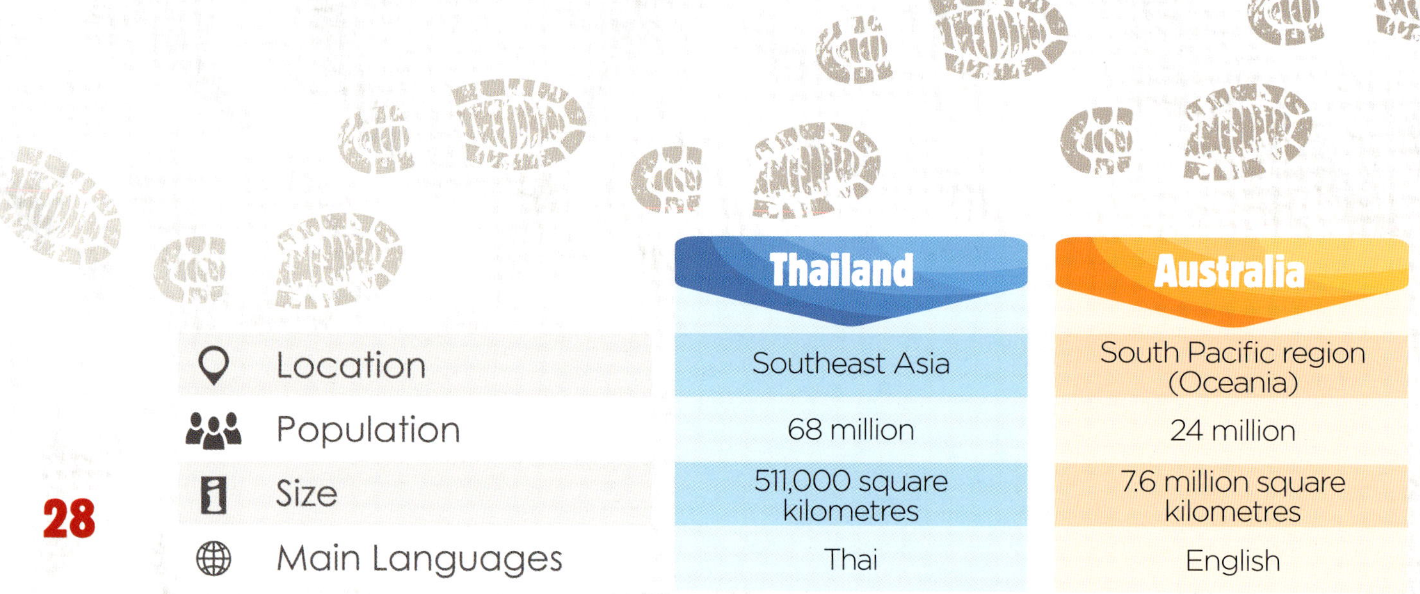

	Thailand	Australia
Location	Southeast Asia	South Pacific region (Oceania)
Population	68 million	24 million
Size	511,000 square kilometres	7.6 million square kilometres
Main Languages	Thai	English

World Geography

Countries of the world are grouped into geographic regions. The main ones are:

Europe, Middle East, Asia, Southeast Asia, Pacific, Oceania, the Americas, North America, Africa

Political and religious events have resulted in some countries being classed in different regions throughout their history. For example, some people place Pakistan in the Middle East, while others locate it in Asia.

Royal Thai cuisine

Buddhist Heavenly Queen Temple in the suburb of Footscray, Melbourne

Vietnam

The capital city of Vietnam is Hanoi.

Vietnam War

Before the Vietnam War in the 1960s and 1970s, there were only about 700 Vietnamese people living in Australia.

The 137,000 Vietnamese asylum seekers who arrived in Australia after the end of the Vietnam War in 1975 were the first large-scale arrivals to come after the White Australia Policy ended. Some came as boat people, while others were selected from refugee camps in Southeast Asian countries. After the 1980s, family reunion became the Australian government's focus for Vietnamese people seeking to live in Australia.

People Today

Vietnamese people form the sixth largest migrant group in Australia. The majority of people with Vietnamese heritage have settled in New South Wales and Victoria.

The communities which grew in the suburbs near the migrant hostels in Sydney and Melbourne are often referred to as 'Little Saigons'. They have become tourist attractions.

Vietnamese Culture

Food

Modern Vietnamese cuisine includes both the traditional fresh ingredients that visitors to Vietnamese restaurants love to enjoy, as well as food that has been influenced by Vietnam's history as a French colony. Vietnamese pastries and bread have a distinct French style.

Religion

There are many religions in Vietnam, including Buddhism, Christianity and the religions of the various ethnic groups. Ceremonies which show respect for and remembrance of ancestors are widely practised.

Festivals

Tet New Year	The date of this traditional spring festival changes each year.
Wandering Souls' Day	Held in the seventh month of the year to pay respect to ancestors

	Vietnam	Australia
Location	Southeast Asia	South Pacific region (Oceania)
Population	95 million	24 million
Size	310,000 square kilometres	7.6 million square kilometres
Main Languages	Vietnamese	English

White Australia Policy

From 1901 to 1973, immigration to Australia was restricted by the White Australia Policy. The Australian government wanted to maintain Australia as an outpost of Great Britain, with a British culture and a population which was mostly British. Multiculturalism was not acceptable, and migrants from Europe were expected to assimilate, so that the British traditions that most Australians treasured would not be lost.

Migrants from Asia and other non-European places were thought to be too different in appearance and culture to ever be able to assimilate and make a contribution to the nation. In addition, Australian workers feared losing their jobs to people who might accept lower wages.

With increases in world travel, and the role of television and other mass media in increasing public awareness, Australia recognised that migrants from many countries would be able to settle harmoniously in Australia and contribute to its economy.

Visit these websites to find out more:

www.migrationheritage.nsw.gov.au
www.emelbourne.net.au
www.sbs.com.au/immigrationnation

Glossary

Consul	a diplomat who supports their nation's citizens living in another country
cuisine	style of cooking
free trade agreement	agreement between countries that makes import and export of goods and services easier
infrastructure	organisations, buildings and equipment needed for a large project
property title	confirmation of ownership of a property
trepang	marine creature, also called a sea cucumber, that is a prized food in many Asian countries
war brides	women who married or became engaged to Australian members of the armed forces overseas during wartime

---

Index

ASEAN 15
asylum seekers 4,8,20,26,30
BRIDGE Project 12
Ceylon 26
Colombo Plan 6,18,27
dragon dance 9
Indochina 6
refugees 7,10,14,20,30
geographic regions 29
Siam 28
White Australia Policy 7,12,14,16,25,30,31
world cultures 19